Chicago Writer **Books**

A Guide to

Writing

Jobs in

Chicago

3e

- ✓ The reality of the marketplace
- ✓ Qualifications, skills, and training required to get the job you want and to stay at the top of your field

Acknowledgements

iWrite Publications Inc. gratefully acknowledges all of the people who took the time to answer our questions. It is their efforts that make this guide valuable to the readers.

Chicago Writer

Keep up-to-date with issues that affect writers, editors, and publishing professionals in Chicago.
Visit our web site at http://www.ChicagoWriter.com.

Published by:
iWrite Publications Inc.
PO Box 10923, Chicago, IL 60610-0923
USA

ISBN 13: 978-1-933048-35-2

Good luck in your writing career!

Contents

Advertising Copywriter

Overview

Definition: Advertising copywriters prepare text for use by publications and broadcast media to promote the sale of goods and services. Copywriters craft words into ideas, images, and concepts that motivate the reader to act.

Reality: Overall, there will be an increase in employment opportunity due to expanding media, but competition is and will continue to be intense.

 High earnings potential for outstanding writers.

 Long hours; demanding clients. Very often, the financial fate of an entire agency depends on the continued satisfaction of one big client.

Qualifications/Skills/Training

Education: Usually requires college degree, often related experience (internships, volunteer work) gives entry-level candidates an edge. Some markets require advanced degrees due to the highly technical nature of the products.

Required Skill Sets: High level of creativity; strong communication and sales skills.

Ongoing Training: Advanced degree or years of support work to get into technical fields; continual refining of writing skills; awareness of new markets, media and technology.

Career Particulars

Types of Organizations That Hire: Ad agencies, corporations, newspapers, magazines, book publishers and public relations companies. Not-for-profit agencies often look for copywriters to write public service announcements promoting their issues. Catalog sales companies hire copywriters. Many consumer goods corporations also have in-house advertising teams. Try: *Leo Burnett, J. Walter Thompson, Chicago Creative Partnership, Grant/Jacoby, CDW Computer Centers, Inc. (catalog operations).*

Job Titles: Copywriter, Promotions Writer, Communications Writer

Salary Range: Entry level: $38,000–$47,000; experienced: $75,000–$95,000

Professional Support

Professional Organizations: American Advertising Federation, American Marketing Association

Professional Publications: *Ad Age*

Résumé Tips

1. **Use clean readable design.**
   Employers are now receiving hundreds of résumés for every job opening they list. Don't make them have to hunt for information. Highlight the most important information about your work, skills, and educational experience—important to the employer.

2. **Use action words.**
   Say that you *wrote* a procedure or *designed* a brochure, or even that you *assisted* with a training script. Using active language gives your résumé a punch of energy and allows employers to separate those that do from those that watch.

3. **Consider your résumé a sales tool.**
   You might want to look through a few books on advertising copywriting to get some ideas about creating interest, using power words, and persuading readers to act.

4. **Analyze job ads and descriptions to identify key words.**
   How much easier would it be to hire you if the employer could read your résumé and have it reflect the key words, phrasing, and skill requirements of the job description he's trying to fill?

5. **Prioritize the content of your résumé.**
   For each entry, list the most important (to the job for which you're applying) or largest impact activity first, rather than the tasks you performed most frequently or the items that were important in your previous position.

Author: Nonfiction

Overview

Definition: Of the almost 200,000 books published each year, more than 80% of them are nonfiction. Nonfiction authors write books across many subgenres such as: art, cookbooks, history, hobbies, how-to, psychology, reference, technology, and self help.

Reality: This is where most authors make money. If you can find a niche and are good at explaining or expressing information that others need, the sky's the limit as far as salability.

	High earnings potential for outstanding writers.
	Few nonfiction books get the huge publicity budgets and glamour of bestselling fiction.

Qualifications/Skills/Training

Education: Education credentials of the writer depend on the subject matter. Readers look for "specialist" credentials in the specific information niche.

Required Skill Sets: High level of creativity; strong communication and sales skills.

Ongoing Training: Continual refining of writing skills; awareness of new markets, media and technology.

Career Particulars

Types of Organizations That Hire: n/a. Authors
contact publishing companies either directly or through literary agents
to propose their book ideas. If publisher is interested, a contract will be
offered to the author.

Job Titles: Author

Salary Range: Compensation is based on advances and/or
royalties negotiated in publishing contract.

Professional Support

Professional Organizations: PEN America, The Authors
Guild, International Women Writers Guild.

Professional Publications: *Writer's Digest, Poets &
Writers, Writer.*

Job Search Notes

_____

_____

_____

_____

_____

_____

_____

_____

_____

_____

_____

_____

_____

_____

Book Reviewer

Overview

Definition: Book reviewers receive free copies of books that they read and write about. Reviewers generally work for a specific publication (newspaper, magazine) or organization (book store, book club).

Reality: Tight market.

	A book lover's dream job. Read an endless stream of free books and broadcast your opinions to the world at large.
	Reviews generally pay by the word. Requires some considerable volume to make a living. Usually done as an adjunct to some related fulltime job.

Qualifications/Skills/Training

Education: Usually requires college degree or expertise in a particular genre. (For instance a trained chef will probably be hired to review cookbooks over a college graduate with a degree in psychology.)

Required Skill Sets: High level of reading comprehension; above average analytical and critical review skills.

Ongoing Training: Continual refinement of writing skills; writing workshops/seminars.

Career Particulars

Types of Organizations That Hire: Consumer
magazines, trade magazines—both technical and professional;
newspapers, web sites. Book stores, book clubs (such as Book of the
Month), and literary organizations also hire. Try: *Chicago Tribune,
Chicago Sun-Times, American Library Association.*

Job Titles: Reviewer, Editor, Senior Editor, Associate Editor, and
Specialty Editor

Salary Range: Freelance reviews pay $.10–$1.50 per word;
with salaried positions, book reviews are usually part of other fulltime
responsibilities.

Professional Support

Professional Organizations: National Book Critics Circle,
Women's National Book Association

Professional Publications: *Pages, Publishers Weekly*

The Number 1 Purpose of a Résumé

The résumé is a tool with one specific purpose:
to win an interview.

Some tips:

- Target your résumés and cover letters to the job and organization you want. Address the specific skills each employer requests.

- Create a résumé that reflects an image to match the salary you want. Many people today are switching careers, reentering the job market after a lapse, or looking for a full-time position after years of part-time work.

  No matter your situation, your goal is to find a job at a salary at least as much as you are now making—or much better!

- Don't limit yourself to one résumé. Create one for each industry or type of job you are seeking.

Business Writer

Overview

Definition: Business writers develop original nonfiction for internal or external books, manuals, trade journals, online publications, company newsletters, radio, TV, video training, or informational brochures.

Reality: As business becomes more globally interconnected, corporations will communicate more through more varied channels. Business writers will be integrated into many departments within organizations as well as developing into entities of their own.

	High earnings potential for outstanding writers. Can move into management.
	Much business writing is technical in nature and internal to the organization. This is not a glamour field.

Qualifications/Skills/Training

Education: Usually requires college degree, often related experience (internships, volunteer work) gives entry-level candidates an edge. Some markets require advanced degrees due to the highly technical nature of the products or the competitive nature of the industry.

Required Skill Sets: Ability to learn concepts quickly and communicate them in simple, clear language. Must be able to take a subject from start to finish: research, interview, organize and convey information, revise, and rewrite—all under project deadline and budget parameters.

Ongoing Training: Continuing education in the field of expertise as well as technical innovations in communications software and media.

Career Particulars

Types of Organizations That Hire: Corporations. Try:
Salton, Inc., American Pharmaceutical Partners, Inc., RC2 Corporation, Hewitt Associates, Alberto-Culver Co., Exelon Corporation, Quotesmith.com Inc., Lifeway Foods Inc., Whitehall Jewelers Inc.

Job Titles: Writer, Communications Specialist, Editor, Communications Manager

Salary Range: $20,000–$80,000; average: $42,000; management $74,000–$99,000

Professional Support

Professional Organizations: International Association of
Business Communicators (IABC), Association for Women in Communications, Society of American Business Editors & Writers

Professional Publications: general business publications.

Résumé Dos and Donts

DO list all relevant work experience.

If your first job out of college was in a support role and you spent grueling months filing employee accident claims, but the in last three weeks you were there you produced a new employee training guide, DO include that job experience. It doesn't matter if that's the only accomplishment you list for that job entry; it counts. (You don't have to tell the interviewer you were chosen because you were the only one who could get the alphabet right!)

DON'T let your résumé go beyond two pages.

Unless you've brokered Middle East peace or perfected nuclear fusion, you haven't accomplished enough to have more than two pages to your résumé. In fact, unless you've been working more than ten years, keep the résumé to one page. Think about how impressed the employer will be with your editing skills!

DO use a simple, clean format.

Use bold type or a slightly larger font to emphasize sections of information. Indent where it will help the reader find data. Generally limit the number of typefaces used to two and don't go smaller than 8pt font.

DON'T add unprofessional personal touches.

Review résumés for any length of time and you'll wonder how some people get jobs at all. Like the financial writer who printed his résumé on graph paper or the marketing writer who printed her photo on one-inch square labels and whenever she listed an important accomplishment, she added a picture of herself winking at the reader. Just don't.

Children's Book Writer

Overview

Definition: Author who writes fiction or nonfiction for the juvenile or young adult market.

Reality: Highly competitive field. Creativity is a must and the ability to accurately judge the comprehension and interests of the age group to which you are writing is essential

 Set your own hours and environment. Allow your creativity to run wild. Growing market.

 Very competitive market. Many magazines and book publishers accept manuscripts only on request or from agents.

Qualifications/Skills/Training

Education: No particular level of education required.

Required Skill Sets: Excellent writing skills and ability to understand and relate to the specific market.

Ongoing Training: Continual refinement writing skills with workshops, seminars, and industry conferences. Attend BookExpo to research what's selling in children's books.

Career Particulars

Types of Organizations That Hire: Writers sell work to juvenile and young adult magazines and book publishers.

Job Titles: Author, Freelance Writer

Salary Range: Compensation is based on advances and/or royalties negotiated in publishing contract.

Professional Support

Professional Organizations: Children's Book Council, Society of Children's Book Writers & Illustrators.

Professional Publications: *Writer's Digest, Writer, Publishers Weekly*

Columnist

Overview

Definition: A writer in a magazine, newspaper, or other publication who has regular space to fill and/or topic to cover. Can range from reporting on advances in appliance manufacturing to local dining experiences.

Reality: The big money is in syndication whereby publications throughout the country pay to include your column in their papers/magazines/web sites. Pay is generally geared to popularity/importance of the column or favorite columnists in popular consumer magazines

 High earnings potential for syndicated writers.

 Difficult to get syndicated.

Qualifications/Skills/Training

Education: Generally high school diploma with experience in niche or bachelor's degree.

Required Skill Sets: Good writing skills, ability to meet deadlines and generate a continuing stream of interesting articles.

Ongoing Training: Writing workshops and seminars; keeping up with changes/advances in the column's topic/industry.

Career Particulars

Types of Organizations That Hire: Consumer
magazines, trade magazines, technical & professional journals,
newspapers, newsletters, web sites.

Job Titles: Editor, Syndicated Columnist, Industry Editor

Salary Range: $25,000–$50,000 for staff positions, additional
for syndicated columnists

Professional Support

Professional Organizations: Society of American
Business Editors & Writers, American Society of Journalists & Authors,
National Writers Union, Society of Professional Journalists.

Professional Publications: *Columbia Journalism Review,
Quill.*

Eight Questions to Expect in a Job Interview

1. In what way do you think you can contribute to our company?

2. What are your short- and long-term goals?

3. What is your greatest strength?
   What is your biggest weakness?

4. What makes you a good team leader?

5. How do you handle conflict?

6. How long do you expect to stay in this job?

7. What do you know about our company?

8. Why should we hire you for this position?

Plus, the clincher...

Do you have any questions for me?

Corporate Communications Writer

Overview

Definition: Those in corporate communications are business writers who specialize in internal and external communications that represent and reflect their companies' images and missions. They produce annual reports, business letters, collateral materials, company newsletters, corporate websites, and press materials.

Reality: Growing market as companies become more global and need to communicate worldwide across all media.

	High growth field with increasing domestic and international opportunities.
	Competitive, high-energy field. Requires commitment and adaptability.

Qualifications/Skills/Training

Education: Bachelor's degree or better; related experience gives candidates an edge.

Required Skill Sets: Ability to express concepts across wide range of audiences. Top writing skills, good business sense, and corporate image and mindset.

Ongoing Training: Continued refinement of writing and business skills.

Career Particulars

Types of Organizations That Hire: Corporations. Try: *Boeing Co., Kraft Foods, Walgreen Co., Sara Lee Corporation, AAR Corporation, Hartmarx Corporation, Tootsie Roll Industries Inc., McDonald's Corporation, Packaging Corporation of America.*

Job Titles: Writer, Corporate Communications Specialist, and Communications Manager

Salary Range: $49,000–$64,000 for smaller organizations; $86,000–$108,000 for those with very high skill levels/experience; $93,000–$118,000 for experienced managers

Professional Support

Professional Organizations: International Association of Business Communicators (IABC), Association of Women in Communications, Society of American Business Editors & Writers.

Professional Publications: general business publications, *Corporate Writer & Editor, Intercom.*

Eight Great Questions to Ask in an Interview

1. What's the makeup of the team as far as experience?

2. What does your company value the most?

3. What skills are you looking for from me to round out the team?

4. What's the most important thing I can do to help within the first 90 days of my employment?

5. Do you have any questions or concerns about my ability to perform this job?

6. When top performers leave the company, why do they leave and where do they usually go?

7. What do you see in me? Do you have any concerns that I need to clear up in order to be the top candidate?

8. Can I meet some members of the team/department?

And Some Not-So-Great Ones

1. What is it that your company does again?

2. What are your psychiatric benefits?

3. Is it difficult to get fired here?

4. Would anyone notice if I came in late and left early?

5. What is the zodiac sign of the company president?

6. How do you define sexual harassment?

7. Will my office be near a soda machine?

Editor

Overview

Definition: Editors review, rewrite, and revise the work of writers and/or other editors. They may also do original writing. Whether a book or magazine editor, their work consists of planning the content of the publication, deciding what material will appeal to the audience, reviewing and editing drafts, and many also oversee the production of the publication.

Reality: Many fine writers find that, over time, they don't enjoy the demands of putting words on a blank screen day after day. With a gift for language, many develop into exemplary editors, working to produce exceptional products in collaboration with writers.

 Growth outlook is optimistic through 2010. Due to electronic text processing, many can telecommute.

 Many editors are overworked because volume increases faster than personnel are added. Not an especially high-paying field.

Qualifications/Skills/Training

Education: College degree usually in communications, journalism, or English.

Required Skill Sets: Ability to express ideas clearly and logically. Must be creative, curious, and self-motivating; able to meet deadlines and budget constraints. Must have an eye for details.

Ongoing Training: Grammar/usage refreshers; keep up with word processing technology.

Career Particulars

Types of Organizations That Hire: Newspapers, magazines, newsletters, book publishers, broadcasting companies, ad agencies, and public relations firms.

Job Titles: Editor, Associate Editor, Managing Editor, and Assistant Editor

Salary Range: $40,000–$60,000 for experienced editors; $68,000–$98,000 for senior positions; $76,000–$98,000 for managing editors

Professional Support

Professional Organizations: American Society of Magazine Editors, Editorial Freelance Association, Association for Women in Communications.

Professional Publications: *CopyEditor, Editorial Eye, Intercom.*

The Art of the Cover Letter

1. **The first rule of cover letters for writers is: no typos!**
   No employer should hire a writer whose résumé or cover letter includes typos, misspelled words, or grammatical errors. Review your letter carefully before sending it out. Don't assume that your spell checker knows the difference between "heard" and "herd," as in "I herd about your job opening...."

2. **Personalize your cover letters.**
   Cover letters should not look like a mass mailing with a "Dear Sir or Madam" at the top. Make every effort to secure the name and correct address of your contact. If you are responding to an advertisement and do not know a specific name, use the contact's title in the greeting, as "Dear Human Resources Manager" or "Dear Recruiter."

3. **Selectively drop names.**
   If an employee in the company or a friend of the recruiter suggested you send the letter, mention that. Hiring managers take résumés with personal associations more seriously than those without connections. Also mention if you've had any personal contact with the addressee. For instance, mention that you met her briefly at the last writing conference or were impressed with the presentation she gave at the mid-season association meeting. That will also let the reader know that you are interested enough in your career to get out and make contacts.

4. **Summarize your assets.**
   Use a paragraph or two to summarize your qualifications for the job opening and your fit with the organization. Be concise. This is the "teaser" section to entice the reader to review your résumé.

5. **Call to action.**
   The closing paragraph of your cover letter should be a brief thank you to the reader for her time and a suggestion of the next course of action. If you are planning a follow-up phone call for the next week, indicate that. Minimally, let the reader know that you look forward to hearing from him soon.

Financial Writer

Overview

Definition: Financial writers write either as employees or freelancers for a financial institution or market. Financial writing must often meet SEC or accounting guidelines in addition to being accurate and understandable.

Reality: A subset of business writing, financial writers must have an understanding and ability to deal with numbers.

 Above average growth expected through 2010.

 One of the most structured writing fields. Need an aptitude for both words and numbers.

Qualifications/Skills/Training

Education: College degree or better with a facile understanding of accounting, economics, banking, or the financial markets.

Required Skill Sets: Ability to express ideas clearly and logically.

Ongoing Training: Continual refinement of writing skills; writing workshops/seminars. Keep up with changes requirements for financial writing/reporting.

Career Particulars

Types of Organizations That Hire: Banks, financial
institutions, financial markets. Try: *Bank of America, Northern Trust, CNA, Household Finance, Chicago Board of Trade, Chicago Mercantile Exchange, Nuveen Investments Inc., William Blair & Co. LLC, Van Kampen Investments, Ariel Capital Management Inc., Heitman Financial LLC.*

Job Titles: Writer, Financial Writer, Manager, and
Communications Specialist

Salary Range: $39,000–$118,000 depending on credentials and
experience

Professional Support

Professional Organizations: American Bankers
Association, Institute for Financial Education, Financial Women International, Society of Professional Journalists, International Association of Business Communicators.

Professional Publications: general business publications,
Intercom, Quill.

Job Search Notes

_____

_____

_____

_____

_____

_____

_____

_____

_____

_____

_____

_____

Ghostwriter

Overview

Definition: Ghostwriters write anything from an article to an entire book for individuals who do not have the time or the ability to do the writing, but have the credentials or expertise in the topic of the work.

Reality: Ghostwriters receive no credit for doing the work. They're hired and get paid; the employer gets his/her name on the finished product.

 Good growth field. As professionals look to publications to boost their credentials, ghostwriters come in demand to produce the products.

 Ego-free zone. You might be busy and you may eventually get paid well, but you get no credit for what you produce.

Qualifications/Skills/Training

Education: College degree or better, depending on the writing niche.

Required Skill Sets: Ability to research, express ideas clearly, and meet deadlines. Must be able to work well with sometimes-temperamental clients.

Ongoing Training: Continual refinement of writing skills; writing workshops/seminars.

Career Particulars

Types of Organizations That Hire: Professional associations, trade publishers, and, sometimes, corporations.

Job Titles: Ghostwriter

Salary Range: n/a. Ghostwriters are paid by the word or project. Rates are generally negotiated with the publisher or client directly. Amounts vary by size of project, writing specialty, and experience of writer (how successful previous books have been).

Professional Support

Professional Organizations: National Writers Union, American Medical Writers Association, Society of Technical Communication.

Professional Publications: *Writer's Digest, Publishers Weekly, Writer.*

Grant Writer

Overview

Definition: Develops resources, researches funding sources, and writes proposals to a variety of organizations. Prepares contract proposals and may administer major contracts. Also may negotiate contractual provisions with potential partners. Has knowledge of standard concepts, practices, and procedures within a particular field.

Reality: Relies on limited experience and judgment to plan and accomplish goals. Performs a variety of tasks. Works under general supervision; typically reports to a manager or head of a unit/department.

 Combines making a living with making a difference. As government money decreases, need for grant writers increases.

 Most not-for-profits work on shoestring budgets. Staff positions disappear when budgets get tight.

Qualifications/Skills/Training

Education: Requires a bachelor's degree in a related area (communications, journalism, English, or liberal arts) and at least three years of work experience.

Required Skill Sets: Ability to write persuasive text within set guidelines and meet deadlines.

Ongoing Training: Continual refinement of writing skills; writing workshops/seminars; grant writing seminars.

Career Particulars

Types of Organizations That Hire: Not-for-profit
organizations, universities. Try: *Donor's Forum, Juvenile Diabetes Foundation, Chicago Historical Society, Roosevelt University.*

Job Titles: Grant Writer

Salary Range: $41,000–$50,000

Professional Support

Professional Organizations: Writing organizations for
camaraderie and support; philanthropic organizations for networking.

Professional Publications: *Writer, CopyEditor, Chronicle of Philanthropy, Philanthropy Magazine.*

Success at Job Fairs

Job fairs are becoming a common means of entry level recruiting. For the corporate recruiter, they offer an opportunity to reach interviewing terminal velocity—the highest possible number of prospects in the shortest possible amount of time. For many students, job fairs provide a "freebie" opportunity to meet with hiring employers.

However, unless you do your homework, you will end up wasting your time at a job fair. Job fairs are the meat markets of the entry level job market, with employers sizing up candidates quickly, based on appearances and first impressions.

Job fairs have a set of rules and protocols all their own. But if you understand how to effectively work within the system, you can easily double or triple your productivity and effectiveness.

Usually a full 50 percent or more of the attendees at job fairs are "window shoppers" who are just browsing to see what is available.

While this approach may seem valid, take note that job fairs are not a "get acquainted session" for you to meet prospective employers. They are multiple interview sessions where the plain vanilla candidates are stepped on and over by those who are targeted and prepared. Yes, even the two- to three-minute greeting and exchange of sound bites is considered a real interview.

You are being evaluated, whether it is for thirty seconds or thirty minutes. You always need to be at your very best. If you are to succeed at the job fair of the new millennium, you have to take a very aggressive yet structured approach.

Indexer

Overview

Definition: Indexers are the organizational minds behind the products coming from nonfictions and scholarly publishers. They evaluate the material and create the sometimes-lengthy indices.

Reality: Indexers must be able to grasp the book's content quickly and produce detailed indexes accurately within project deadlines.

 Follows the demand for nonfiction and scholarly books. Growth expected through 2010.

 Work can be tedious for those who do not have a strong ability for maintaining consistency and noticing details.

Qualifications/Skills/Training

Education: College degree or better, depending on the writing niche.

Required Skill Sets: Ability to research, understand complex ideas, and meet deadlines. Must be extremely detail oriented.

Ongoing Training: Continual refinement of indexing skills; workshops/seminars.

Career Particulars

Types of Organizations That Hire: Professional associations, trade publishers, scholarly publishers, and, sometimes, corporations.

Job Titles: Indexer

Salary Range: Most indexers are freelancers. Compensation depends on indexer's educational background, experience, and size of project.

Professional Support

Professional Organizations: National Writers Union, American Medical Writers Association, Society for Technical Communication, National Association of Indexers.

Professional Publications: *Writer's Digest, Publishers Weekly, Writer.*

Legal Writer

Overview

Definition: Legal writers develop legal or legislative materials such as reports, analyses, briefs, articles, and translations for non-legal readers.

Reality: The primary job of the legal writer is to transform legal information and jargon into material that is understandable to the target audience.

 Above average growth through 2010. As legal activity shows no signs of slowing, more people are interested in the proceedings and outcomes.

 Although legal writers are rarely out of work, this is not a glamour job. This is a behind-the-scenes job generating information people need, but don't necessarily want to read.

Qualifications/Skills/Training

Education: College degree as well as some degree of expertise in subject matter. Many positions require a law degree, but not necessarily admittance to the bar.

Required Skill Sets: Logical mind, excellent writing skills, ability to describe complex subject matter in simple terms.

Ongoing Training: Continual refinement of writing skills; writing workshops/seminars; continued training in field of expertise.

Career Particulars

Types of Organizations That Hire: Corporations, law firms, military, media firms. Try Sidley Austin Brown & Wood, Kirkland & Ellis, Mayer Brown Rowe & Maw, Winston & Strawn, Jenner & Block, WGN News, WLS News, ABC, CBS, NBC, and cable affiliates, *Chicago Journal of International Law, Chicago Law Journal.*

Job Titles: Legal Writer

Salary Range: $44,000–$88,000; supervisory and management positions, $72,000–$96,000.

Professional Support

Professional Organizations: American Bar Association.

Professional Publications: *Corporate Writer & Editor, Intercom.*

Literary Agent

Overview

Definition: A literary agent represents an author's work to publishers. They work with the author to polish the manuscript, then "shop" it to those publishing houses that would most likely be interested.

Reality: Literary agents often act as sales representatives for an author's manuscripts and nursemaid for the author. A good agent can make the difference between get published and languishing in the slush pile on an editor's desk.

 Some growth expected as large publisher rely more on agented work and niche publishers continuously spring up.

 Strictly commission sales. Until you build up a selling clientele, income can be slim.

Qualifications/Skills/Training

Education: No particular education requirements. Experience and contacts in the publishing industry are more important.

Required Skill Sets: Ability to detect trends in publishing; good sales and marketing skills; ability to work with sometimes-temperamental writers.

Ongoing Training: Writing workshops/seminars; Book Expo.

Career Particulars

Types of Organizations That Hire: Literary agents are freelance or work for agency firms.

Job Titles: Literary Agent

Salary Range: Generally, agents earn 15% of the income for works they represent.

Professional Support

Professional Organizations: Association of Authors Representatives.

Professional Publications: *Writer's Digest, Publishers Weekly, Writer.*

Magazine Feature Writer

Overview

Definition: Feature writers generate longer, special interest articles for newspapers and magazines. Subject matter is usually determined by world events, seasonal activities, industry trends, etc.

Reality: Opportunities abound for writers to create feature stories on a wide variety of topics. Writers can specialize in one area of interest or industry or write about what catches their interest.

 Growth through 2010. Magazines and e-magazines are starting up and expanding content.

 Until a writer makes a name or establishes a niche, can get as many articles turned down as accepted.

Qualifications/Skills/Training

Education: Generally high school diploma with experience in niche or bachelor's degree.

Required Skill Sets: Good writing skills, ability to meet deadlines and generate a continuing stream of interesting articles.

Ongoing Training: Continual refinement of writing skills; writing workshops/seminars; keeping up with changes/advances in the column's topic/industry.

Career Particulars

Types of Organizations That Hire: Consumer, association and trade magazines; newspapers; publicists may hire outside writers to write profiles on their clients.

Job Titles: Feature Writer, Columnist, Editor

Salary Range: Salaries for full-time employees are based on complete job position, see *Editor, Columnist,* and *News Reporter,* freelance rates can run from $.10 per word to several thousand dollars per article based on the size of the publication and qualifications of the writer.

Professional Support

Professional Organizations: American Society of Magazine Editors, Society of Professional Journalists.

Professional Publications: *Byline, Editorial Eye, Quill.*

Networking Basics

1. **Network everyday, everywhere.**
   Follow the demand for your talent by continuous networking, making it second nature. Make your own connections and be your own agent.

   Keep communication open with past employers and clients, being careful not to burn bridges when you leave a company. If you leave the workforce for a few years to raise children, network with other stay-at-home parents and attend your partner's company events at the holidays.

2. **Keep your résumé current.**
   Many people leave updating their résumés until they're in an active job search. That's too late in the game. By always having a current résumé, you can more easily provide contacts with brief synopses of your accomplishments. Create a version of your résumé for networking alone, one that can be pulled out on short notice.

3. **Use informational interviews.**
   Exploit another networking staple with an informational interview—a formal chat in which you ask someone to talk about his or her work without trying to squeeze a job out of the experience. It can be a particularly useful way to get a detailed picture of the industry since you are free to ask absolutely anything and can more often expect a frank response than in a regular interview.

4. **Network toward a job.**
   When you actively start to look for work, contact everyone you know. Go to your immediate and extended family, friends of the family, religious community, volunteer connections, old college buddies or clubs, past employers, and anyone you deal with including your accountant, real estate agent, or dentist. Reciprocate when they call you.

5. **Put your network to use.**
   References can have a significant impact on the final hiring decision. Be ready to provide potential employers with at least three solid ones from your network of professional contacts.

Medical Writer

Overview

Definition: Medical writers present detailed information on the physical or medical sciences and explain research findings for scientific or medical professions. They often interpret medical or scientific information for a general readership.

Reality: There is a great demand for qualified medical writers, both in industry and advertising. Medical information geared to a general readership is a new and rapidly growing niche.

	Exceptional growth expected.
	Highly technical information does not appeal to everyone. Requires commitment to keep up-to-date on scientific and medical developments.

Qualifications/Skills/Training

Education: College education or better. For many positions, employers are looking for post-graduate and doctoral understanding of subject matter.

Required Skill Sets: Ability to explain complex information in an easily understood language. Research skills are also required.

Ongoing Training: Continuing education in specialty; writing seminars and workshops.

Career Particulars

Types of Organizations That Hire: Corporations,
medical advertising firms, medical and scientific associations. Try:
*Baxter International Inc., Option Care, Inc., Stericycle Inc., Abbott
Laboratories Inc., Rhea & Kaiser Marketing Communications Inc.,
Chicago Creative Partnership, A. Eicoff & Co.*

Job Titles: Medical Writer, Science Writer, Technical Writer

Salary Range: $40,000–$90,000, depending on experience;
supervisory positions and management can make $72,000–$96,000.

Professional Support

Professional Organizations: American Medical Writers
Association, National Association of Science Writers.

Professional Publications: *Writer, InterCom.*

Networking Success

Take networking seriously. Don't spread the meetings with your list of contacts out over a month-long period. Start on a Monday morning and call everyone to book a get-together for later in the week or at the latest, early next week.

When you have the meeting, keep it light. Don't show up with your résumé and ask, "Do you know of any jobs?" This is simply a reconnaissance mission. The person you're having coffee with is in the business and knows what's happening. Ask for this information. Try saying something as simple and straightforward as: "You're plugged into what's going on around town. Any suggestions on whom I can talk to about what might be coming up in the future?"

Get three names from each contact. By the end of the week, you may have a couple of dozen names of people in the industry. Sit down the next Monday morning and call them. Introduce yourself, explain where you got their names and ask if you can have fifteen minutes of their time. Suggest meeting for a coffee near their office. Often, the person will say something like, "Why don't you drop in around 3PM. We can talk here in my office."

Schedule your week, filling in time slots to meet people. And again, get three names from each of these people. After a while, you may notice an overlapping of names as your contacts give you names of people you have already contacted.

Don't ask for a job. Just the same as meeting with your acquaintances, keep it light. Say that you're looking for a place in the industry and in the meantime, you're making an all-out effort to keep plugged into what's happening.

Ascertain, if possible, what interests the people you meet. Keep a record of whom you met and what their interests are. This gives you a good opening for re-contacting them if you see an article or hear about something that might interest them. Keep in gentle contact with them.

You not only get your name spread around town so that when something does come up in your line of work you hear about it, there are ancillary benefits to this kind of dedicated and aggressive networking. You get to meet a wide variety of interesting people and your keep your working muscles intact by having a specific task to do each week: meet more contacts.

News Reporter

Overview

Definition: Reporters investigate leads and new tips; observe and interview people in the news; and organize materials to determine the focus or emphasis of their stories.

Reality: Above average growth expected through 2010. Takes many years of covering minor events to make a name for oneself in this field.

By breaking news stories or providing helpful information, reporters can feel they are making a contribution to society.

Competition is keen. Reporters work irregular hours with frequent night and weekend shifts.

Qualifications/Skills/Training

Education: College degree in journalism and writing experience. Large publications usually require 3–5 years solid experience.

Required Skill Sets: Crisp, concise writing; ability to meet deadlines.

Ongoing Training: Continual refinement of writing skills; writing workshops/seminars.

Career Particulars

Types of Organizations That Hire: Large city daily
newspapers or suburban and small town dailies or weeklies. Entry jobs
open up most often on smaller publications. Also broadcast media,
online media sites, and wire services have outlets in large cities.

Job Titles: Reporter, Editor

Salary Range: $29,000–$58,000, depending on experience and
size of publication

Professional Support

Professional Organizations: Illinois Women's Press
Association, Society of American Business Editors & Writers, The
Reporters' Network, Society of Professional Journalists, Newspaper
Association of America.

Professional Publications: *Press Time*

Evaluating a Job Offer

The search is finally over. You've received a job offer and it sounds too good to be true. Before you scream, "I accept," step back and think. There are many factors to weigh before deciding whether to accept and on what conditions.

When you receive the initial offer, ask for time.

Most employers will not retract the offer if you ask for time to mull it over. Employers should give a minimum of one to two days, but a week is an acceptable request. If potential employers question your motives, explain that you want to make the best decision possible.

The evaluation process begins during the interview. If you requested the right information during the interview, you'll be better equipped to make a decision later.

- **Salary**
  There's more to happiness than money, but bills still have to be paid. Know what others in your field are making by searching a database such as salary.com.

- **The Organization**
  First, research the organization on the company Web site. You can gather basic information during the interview, but be wary of "buzzwords" that recruiters think potential employees want to hear. You can get background on an organization by contacting its public relations office or by exploring the Internet.

  Long-term projections for a company's industry can provide a good indicator for the future of your job. Check out the Bureau of Labor Statistics' projections of employment and output for more than 200 industries.

  The *Occupational Outlook Handbook* from the Department of Labor Statistics also provides job outlook and earnings information. The handbook recommends additional criteria to consider, such as weighing small firms against large ones and established organizations against start-ups.

Novelist

Overview

Definition: Novelists create original works of fiction for publication.

Reality: Although millions of books are sold each year, both in print and electronically, writing fiction is still a risky way to make a living. Few break though the bestseller lists.

 Exercise your creativity. Plan your own hours.

 Income is erratic. Work can be isolating. High competition for publisher's attention and publicity dollars for non-bestselling books.

Qualifications/Skills/Training

Education: n/a

Required Skill Sets: Ability to write creatively and meet agreed-to deadlines.

Ongoing Training: Continual refinement of writing skills; writing workshops/seminars.

Career Particulars

Types of Organizations That Hire: n/a. Novelists sell
manuscripts to publishers or self publish their own works.

Job Titles: Novelist

Salary Range: n/a. Royalties are negotiated per contract and
depend on book niche and previous sales.

Professional Support

Professional Organizations: PEN America, the Authors
Guild, Mystery Writers of America, Romance Writers of America,
International Women Writers Guild.

Professional Publications: *Writer's Digest, Poets &
Writers, Writer, Harper's.*

About Agents

Finding a Literary Agent can be the making of a writing career.

There is more to being a writer than stringing words together. Even great writers have to do more than write.

Unless you can persuade someone to publish the words you slave over, your writing will remain unknown and unread and writing will drain rather than fill your bank account.

That's where a Literary Agent comes in. Your literary agent is the book-marketing expert who can sell your crafted words to jaded publishing professionals. He or she can turn a manuscript gathering dust in your desk drawer into a published book paying the bills. A reputable agent will go to work for you to make sure that your writing pays what it should.

An agent will give your work a much better chance of escaping the slush piles that threaten to overwhelm the office space of all successful publishers. Your job, which isn't easy, is produce writing that an agent can believe in.

Many online directories of literary agents may include agents who charge a reading fee for reviewing a manuscript. This is often considered an indicator of a disreputable agent.

For advice about a particular agent, try querying the Association of Authors Representatives (US) or the Association of Authors Agents (UK). Both organizations have stringent membership requirements that exclude the dubious practices that are a sad fact of the publishing industry.

There are reputable agents who do not belong to these organizations. But any agent whose terms do not fall within the bounds of what these organizations consider acceptable practice should be approached with caution.

Playwright

Overview

Definition: Playwrights write stage plays that will be performed—usually live—by actors.

Reality: Opportunities are tight. Funding is difficult to secure and most plays close before they make money.

 Exercise your creativity. Set your own hours. Receive live audience feedback for your successes.

 Small market. Tight competition. Work can be isolating.

Qualifications/Skills/Training

Education: n/a.

Required Skill Sets: Ability to write creatively in a set format using both description and dialogue.

Ongoing Training: Continual refinement of writing skills; writing workshops/seminars.

Career Particulars

Types of Organizations That Hire: n/a. Playwrights
sell plays to publishers or obtain funding to put on production. Try:
university theatres, community theatres, Chicago theatre groups.

Job Titles: Playwright

Salary Range: n/a. Payment is negotiated with publisher or
funding source.

Professional Support

Professional Organizations: The Dramatist's Guild of
America.

Professional Publications: Scr(i)pt

More about Agents

Getting an agent requires patience, persistence and above all talent. It's not enough to win a few obscure contests or to send a singing telegram. What most agents want from a writer is a great script. Not a good script—a great one.

Research is key in finding a good agent and writers seeking representation should figure out what kinds of scripts interest the agent. You may have many scripts, but it is a good idea to pitch one per query letter. Pick one that you think would appeal to the agent. A query letter has to be short and listing ten scripts would probably make it a two-page letter that will likely end up in the circular file.

Keep in mind that agents get hundreds of letters each week and very few of those letters pitch a script that is remotely interesting. Give agencies at least two to four weeks to reply to your query letter. Calling the agency and bothering them about a query is a waste of time. Save your phone calls for when they request the script and take months to respond.

There are a number of agencies in the Writers Guild List of Agents that try to make a living charging writers fees. Do not pay a dime for representation. WGA signatory agents are not permitted to charge fees for anything. If an agent requests a reading fee, a referral fee, a photocopying fee, a signing fee, etc., do not pay it and report them immediately to the Writers Guild of America.

Query letters are effective in drawing attention to a speculative screenplay; however, the best way to get an agent is by a referral. Someone you know knows someone who knows someone who knows the agent and can get your script directly into the agent's hands. Attend seminars and screenwriting workshops to meet writers and agents. The next best thing is to win one of the top screenwriting contests and have the agents come to you.

Poet

Overview

Definition: Poets write poetry for publication or, sometimes, live production.

Reality: Very small market for poetry. Very few poets write poetry as a fulltime means of income.

 Exercise your creativity. Set your own hours.

 Small market. Low compensation. Work can be isolating.

Qualifications/Skills/Training

Education: n/a

Required Skill Sets: Ability to express yourself creatively in poetry.

Ongoing Training: Continual refinement of writing skills; writing workshops/seminars.

Career Particulars

Types of Organizations That Hire: n/a. Poets sell
their work to magazines and book publishers.

Job Titles: Poet

Salary Range: n/a. Poets negotiate payment with magazines or
publishers.

Professional Support

Professional Organizations: Poetry Club, The
Association of Small Press Poets, Science Fiction Poetry Association.

Professional Publications: *Poetry, Poets & Writers,*
Writer.

Job Search Notes

_____

_____

_____

_____

_____

_____

_____

_____

_____

_____

_____

_____

_____

Proofreader

Overview

Definition: Proofreaders proofread, review, and edit materials for accurate use of grammar and content. They also correct any grammatical, typographical, or compositional errors in original copy.

Reality: Proofreaders should see above average growth through 2010. Requires a keen eye and a passion for details.

 Proofreaders with knowledge of technical or medical style guides and vocabulary have additional opportunities and higher pay open to them.

 It's all in the details. Accuracy is paramount. Can be a dead-end job for those not interested in editorial work.

Qualifications/Skills/Training

Education: May require an associate's degree and 2-4 years of experience in the field or in a related area.

Required Skill Sets: Knowledge of spelling, grammar, and punctuation, as well as style guide used by the client or employer. Must be detail oriented.

Ongoing Training: Grammar refreshers/workshops; changes is usage or style guides.

Career Particulars

Types of Organizations That Hire: Book publishers, magazines, association publishers.

Job Titles: Proofreader

Salary Range: $34,000–$47,700

Professional Support

Professional Organizations: International Association of Business Communicators

Professional Publications: *CopyEditor, Editorial Eye*

Public Relations Specialist /Publicist

Overview

Definition: These writers generate materials that build, maintain, and promote beneficial relationships between organizations and the public they serve.

Reality: PR/Publicity Specialists research and communicate information and issues that assist their employers or clients to win public approval.

 Senior-level specialists can be in high profile, public positions. Job opportunities expected to increase faster than average.

 There's no such thing as bad publicity, except for the publicist. May often end up as the buffer between an angry public and a misbehaving client.

Qualifications/Skills/Training

Education: College degree in communications or public relations. Internship or other related experience helps in entry-level jobs.

Required Skill Sets: Creativity, good judgment, outgoing personality, as well as the ability to write and speak well.

Ongoing Training: Continual refinement of writing skills; writing workshops/seminars; ongoing learning about clients' businesses.

Career Particulars

Types of Organizations That Hire: Corporations, not-for-profits, public relations agencies, tourist attractions, convention planners, restaurants. Try: *Ty, Inc., CF Industries, Hyatt Hotels, Ace Hardware Corporation, Pepper Constructions Group, Navy Pier, area casinos, zoos, sports teams, museums, race tracks, Chicago Cultural Center.*

Job Titles: Publicist, PR Specialist

Salary Range: $39,000–$50,000; those with 7+ years experience, $71,000–$101,000; management in large companies or agencies, $94,000–$110,000.

Professional Support

Professional Organizations: Council of Public Relations Firms, Publicity Club of Chicago, Public Relations Society of America.

Professional Publications: *Ad Age.*

Cover Letter Design

Letterhead

It is so easy to create a letterhead all your own and to make it match your résumé. Just copy into a new document the name and address you have already created for your résumé. It couldn't be simpler! It makes a very sharp impression when your cover letter and résumé match in every respect from paper color to font to letterhead.

Paper

The type of paper (bond, linen, laid, cover stock, or coated) isn't as important, although it also projects an image. Uncoated paper (bond, linen, laid) makes a classic statement. It feels rich and makes people think of corporate stationery and important documents. Coated stock recalls memories of magazines, brochures, and annual reports.

Regardless of the paper you choose, mail your résumé flat instead of folded. It costs a few extra cents in postage and a little more for the 9 × 12 envelope, but the impression it makes is well worth the extra cost. It also helps with the scannability of your résumé.

Thank yous and other follow-up letters can be folded in standard No. 10 business envelopes.

Résumé Writer

Overview

Definition: These writers design effective résumés for customers.

Reality: As employment environment becomes tighter, job seekers look for a competitive edge. Résumés can make the difference between securing an interview and losing an opportunity.

 For effective writers attached to a high-powered search firm, there is always a flow of people changing jobs.

 Need for these writers can fluctuate with the economy. People don't worry about their résumés when there are more jobs than qualified candidates.

Qualifications/Skills/Training

Education: Generally a college degree in a writing discipline or related field.

Required Skill Sets: Ability to describe a client's work history in positive, action-oriented language in a one- to two-page format.

Ongoing Training: Ongoing workshops/seminars on hiring trends.

Career Particulars

Types of Organizations That Hire: Most writers are
freelance or work for recruitment or outplacement firms. Try: *Heidrick & Struggles International Inc., Korn/Ferry International, Russell Reynolds Associates Inc., Callan Associates Ltd., Kennedy & Co., Whitney Group.*

Job Titles: Résumé Writer

Salary Range: $20,000–$59,000

Professional Support

Professional Organizations: Professional Résumé
Writing & Research Association, Professional Association of Résumé Writers, Society for Technical Communication

Professional Publications: *CopyEditor, Editorial Eye.*

Types of Résumés

Chronological Résumé:

The chronological résumé format is typically the most effective type of format as it quickly shows relevant job skills to an employer, thus enhancing the first impression you create.

The chronological résumé format works well if your past employment meets several criteria, including:

- Your work history is related to your current objectives, and ideally shows progressive job responsibility in a specific career direction.

- The amount of experience you have (number of years) falls into an appropriately marketable range.

- You are presently employed or have not been unemployed for a long period of time.

- Your length of employment in each job falls into an acceptable range.

Functional resume:

The functional résumé format presents qualifications that support your current objectives by illustrating only your functional skills. A functional format may show a brief work history at the end of the résumé, but without job descriptions and accomplishments.

The functional résumé format is often used to hide unfavorable elements in a candidate's employment history; therefore human resource professionals might view it with caution.

Combination resume:

The combination résumé format combines the features of the chronological and the functional résumé formats. It allows you to focus more thoroughly on your marketable job skills and qualifications first and foremost before presenting your employment history.

In almost all instances, the combination format is a better choice than a straight functional format. The combination résumé format is also a better choice than the chronological format if your most recent work history is not directly related to your current career goals.

Scriptwriter/Screenplay Writer

Overview

Definition: These writers write scripts for television productions, documentaries, variety show, situation comedies, and corporate uses.

Reality: This field can expect higher than average growth. Despite the fact that entertainment scripts such as movie screenplays get so much attention, there is more work in the business sector (corporations, manufacturing, government, and education).

 Highly creative venue for writers. Talented screenwriters can command big money.

 Highly competitive field. Big money in movies or television requires a move to the Los Angeles area.

Qualifications/Skills/Training

Education: Generally hired based on experience and ability.

Required Skill Sets: Ability to describe both audio and visual elements of a production. Must have an ear for dialogue and knowledge of camera angles, set descriptions, and acting directions for performers.

Ongoing Training: Continual refinement of writing skills; writing workshops/seminars.

Career Particulars

Types of Organizations That Hire: Movie producers, television producers, corporations, and training consulting firms. Try: *Leo Burnet, Helene Curtis, McDonald's Corporation, Motorola, Second City.*

Job Titles: Scriptwriter, Screenwriter

Salary Range: $30,000–$500,000

Professional Support

Professional Organizations: Writer Guild of America, The Scriptwriters Network, CineStory, Chicago Screenwriting Network, American Screenwriters Association.

Professional Publications: *Screenwriter Magazine, Scr(i)pt, ScreenTalk, Creative Screenwriting Magazine.*

Speech Writer

Overview

Definition: This writer prepares and/or writes speeches, briefings, and other documents for key executive corporate positions.

Reality: Tight market for a specialized expertise. Not all good writers can also be good speechwriters.

 Many top executives, public officials, and clients take their speechwriters with them to subsequent positions when the relationship works.

 Big clients can equal big egos. You may have to know how to kowtow as well as you know how to write.

Qualifications/Skills/Training

Education: Generally requires a bachelor's degree in a writing discipline or a related area of expertise. For corporate speechwriter, familiar with a variety of the field's concepts, practices, and procedures is a real plus.

Required Skill Sets: Excellent writing ability with an ear for how the words will sound when spoken; creativity; and an understanding of the speaker's field of expertise.

Ongoing Training: Continual refinement of writing skills; writing workshops/seminars.

Career Particulars

Types of Organizations That Hire: Corporations,
government, independent clients. Try: *Aon Corp., Kraft Foods, Federal Reserve Bank of Chicago, Avon, City of Chicago.*

Job Titles: Speechwriter

Salary Range: $60,000–$78,000

Professional Support

Professional Organizations: National Speakers
Association, Toastmasters International, International Platform Association, National Writers Union.

Professional Publications: *The Executive Speaker, The
"Quote...Unquote" Newsletter, Speechwriter's Newsletter.*

Evaluating a Job Offer, Part 2

No matter how many perks the job offers, you will be unhappy if you dislike the day-to-day work. Ask specifically what the job entails, what your responsibilities will be and what they expect you to contribute to the company. Fancy titles like "administrative distribution technician" may translate to "incoming fax distributor."

Another important factor to consider is the office environment. One of the best ways to get a feel for your new job is too talk to current employees and tour the office.

Consider: hours, attire, office space, coworkers, employers, and whether the organization's interest and beliefs are compatible with your own.

Benefits are an important consideration when deciding on a job, and they vary a great deal from company to company. Sometimes salaries are non-negotiable. If you can't get as much as you think you deserve, you may be able to extract it from signing bonuses, training programs, or reimbursements for moving costs.

Think about mobility. Will there be a chance to move up in the company? Will the skills acquired from your new position contribute to your career overall? Where is the person who had the job before you?

Finally, ask about salary review. Most companies evaluate your performance annually. Are there opportunities for a salary or benefit increase after the first evaluation? If you aren't able to negotiate the starting salary you originally desired, you may have opportunities for salary increases or promotions after the first six months.

Once you've made the big decision, let the employer know politely and as soon as possible. Follow up with a letter. It's important to get things in writing.

Technical Writer

Overview

Definition: Technical writers develop scientific or technical materials such as reports, equipment manuals, operational guides, business process and workflow manuals, and software user guides

Reality: The primary job of the technical writer is to transform technical information and jargon into material that is understandable to the target audience.

 Above average growth through 2010. We are an information society and technical writers are the backbone of factual communication.

 Although technical writers are rarely out of work, this is not a glamour job. This is a behind-the-scenes job generating information people need, but don't necessarily want to read.

Qualifications/Skills/Training

Education: College degree as well as some degree of expertise in subject matter.

Required Skill Sets: Logical mind, excellent writing skills, ability to describe complex subject matter in simple terms.

Ongoing Training: Continual refinement of writing skills; writing workshops/seminars; continued training in field of expertise.

Career Particulars

Types of Organizations That Hire: Corporations, computer-consulting firms, web design firms, military, engineering firms. Try: *CNA Financial Corporation, Kemper Insurance Companies, Motorola Inc., Aon Corp., Borg Warner Inc., Anixter International Inc., US Cellular Corporation, GATX Corporation, Tellabs Inc., Idex Corporation, SPSS Inc., Schawk Inc.*

Job Titles: Technical Writer

Salary Range: $40,000–$80,000; supervisory and management positions, $67,000–$95,000.

Professional Support

Professional Organizations: Society of Technical Communication, Computer Press Association, National Association of Science Writers.

Professional Publications: *Corporate Writer & Editor, Intercom.*

Finding Government Jobs

Jobs exist at the Federal, State, county, city and local government level. Local government jobs may include utilities, schools and hospitals.

Government job opportunities
Opportunities are announced either through a bulletin or job announcement. The opportunities are open either for a given period of time with a closing date, or are
continuous. Continuous opportunities may be closed by the agency at any time.

Job bulletins or announcements are posted at government offices, sometimes published in newspapers, and sometimes posted on the Internet. Identify government jobs openings by:

- Call the government agencies in the city that you're interested in. You can find these agencies by looking in the telephone book. Ask for the personnel or human resources office. Describe your experience and training and ask for help in identifying potential job opportunities.

  If you identify a job opportunity and the agency is not taking applications, you may ask to be notified when applications will be taken by filling out a request. A number of agencies provide e-mail notification.

- Visit the government agencies in the locations that you're interested in. Follow the same steps as you would in calling the agency.

Training Developer

Overview

Definition: Training Developers participate in and conduct adult training programs. They determine training objectives and write training programs, including outlines, text, handouts, tests, and designs laboratory exercises.

Reality: Adult training is a booming field. Many adults now have several careers within a working lifetime and require new training for each. Online training is growing especially fast due to the attraction of distance learning.

 Almost every organization in every industry has training needs.

 Depending on the size of the organization, can be a rigorous job where developer also conducts the live training.

Qualifications/Skills/Training

Education: Generally requires a bachelor's degree in area of training, education, business, or writing discipline.

Required Skill Sets: Familiar with a variety of the field's concepts, practices, and procedures. Relies on experience and judgment to plan and accomplish goals. Requires public speaking ability and leadership.

Ongoing Training: Continued advancement in training field as well as training concepts and tools (software, etc.).

Career Particulars

Types of Organizations That Hire: Colleges, corporations, educational publishers, not-for-profits, adult education and training providers. Try: *Career Education Corporation, Purple Monkey Studios Inc., Discovery Center.*

Job Titles: Trainer, Training Specialist, Training Developer

Salary Range: $25,000–$94,000 for in-house positions, depending on experience and the technical level of the training; freelance trainers, $90,000–125,000.

Professional Support

Professional Organizations: Chicagoland Chapter of the American Society for Training and Development

Professional Publications: *Training Today*

Travel Writer

Overview

Definition: Travel writers deliver the specifics about travel destinations (travel, food, accommodations, sites) to the reading public.

Reality: With a globe on the move, travel writers should experience significant growth through the next decade. Both business and leisure travel levels are now exceeding pre-9/11 highs and with a surge of self-bookings, travelers need information about where to go and stay.

 From world cruises to RVing across the country, there are as many travel writing niches as there are travelers.

 Most travel writing is freelance and not all travel is first class. Your wanderlust has to exceed your comfort needs.

Qualifications/Skills/Training

Education: Generally college-level writing is required if working for an organization.

Required Skill Sets: Ability to describe sites and scenes so that the reader develops a desire to visit—descriptive motivational writing.

Ongoing Training: Continual refinement of writing skills; writing workshops/seminars, lots of travel.

Career Particulars

Types of Organizations That Hire: Travel-industry magazines, travel book publishers, hotel chains, travel web sites, tour companies, newspapers.

Job Titles: Travel Writer

Salary Range: n/a. Most travel writing is freelance. Rates are negotiated based on experience and quality of article. Book contracts are negotiated based on previous sales and book category.

Professional Support

Professional Organizations: International Food, Wine, and Travel Writers Association.

Professional Publications: *Travel Writer Marketletter, Travel Writers Newsletter*.

Business Dining Etiquette

More candidates than you can imagine lose career opportunities because of poor dining etiquette. These skills are especially important in jobs where first impressions can make or break business deals. Some of the rules may seem a bit picky, but attention to details like these can make a difference in how you are perceived by others.

1. When dining with a group, the rule is to drink to your right and eat to your left.

2. As a general rule, use the outer utensils first and work your way to the inner.

3. The dessert fork or spoon is located at the 12 o'clock position above your plate at a formal business dinner.

4. Your hands and arms should be in your lap when you are between bites.

5. Closing your menu signals the waiter that you are ready to order.

6. When choosing what to order, select something you like that is easy to manage.

7. When eating meat, you should cut only enough of the meat for one bite at a time.

8. If you briefly excuse yourself during the meal, place your napkin on the seat or arm of your chair.

9. When you have finished eating, place your utensils in the 10 o'clock to 4 o'clock position across the plate.

10. At the completion of the meal, place your napkin to the right of the place setting. If the plates have been removed, place your napkin in the center.

11. Three things you should always do when meeting someone professionally are: make good eye contact, offer a firm handshake, and smile.

Web Content Writer

Overview

Definition: These writers create marketing or educational information for communication via an organization's web sites.

Reality: Web content writers are the new kids on the block. Current holders of this position have come from writing, editing, marketing, or even programming backgrounds. There is little consistency in skill levels or qualifications yet.

 A growing field as more and more communication is either duplicated on or targeted specifically for the Internet.

 Many organizations still do not know how to hire or what they expect of a web content writer.

Qualifications/Skills/Training

Education: Generally a college degree is expected or experience in the organization's business.

Required Skill Sets: Hybrid writing ability melding technical writing clarity and journalistic terseness. Must also know enough HTML and scripting to markup text to present well online.

Ongoing Training: Continual refinement of writing skills; writing workshops/seminars; classes to keep up with technology.

Career Particulars

Types of Organizations That Hire: Corporations, not-for-profits, .com companies, computer consulting firms, web developers. Try: *Agency.com Ltd., Camino Project Inc., Chicago Systems Group, Hamilton & Bond Advertising, Inc., Intelli.com Inc.*

Job Titles: Web Content Specialist, Web Writer, Webmaster, Online Editor

Salary Range: Web Writer/Content Specialist: $43,000–$88,000; Online Editor: $33,000–$110,000

Professional Support

Professional Organizations: Webgrrls, International Webmaster Association, Women's New Media Alliance, Society for Technical Communication.

Professional Publications: *PC, Corporate Writer & Editor, Intercom.*

Dress for Interview Success

Men and Women

- Conservative business suit with long-sleeved shirt/blouse
- Clean, polished conservative shoes
- Well-groomed hairstyle
- Minimal cologne or perfume
- Light briefcase or portfolio case
- No visible body piercing

Men

- Necktie should be silk with a conservative pattern
- Dark shoes and socks
- Good haircut; short hair always fares best in interviews
- No beards or mustaches; if you must, make sure it is neat and trimmed
- No jewelry other than wedding ring or college ring

Women

- Wear a suit with a jacket; no dresses
- Shoes with conservative heels
- Conservative hosiery at or near skin color
- Carry a briefcase instead of a purse
- If you wear nail polish, use clear or a conservative color
- Minimal use of makeup

Writing Instructor

Overview

Definition: Writing instructors teach anything from basic composition to first-year level students to specialized seminars and workshops on topics such as business writing, scriptwriting, or fiction.

Reality: Internet instruction is expected to increase dramatically due to the draw of distance learning.

 Opportunities expected to grow faster than average due to the influx of students into colleges, continuing education, and making career changes.

 For college educators, tenured professorships are hard to come by. Many institutions have ratios of 3-to-1 part-time instructors to fulltime professors.

Qualifications/Skills/Training

Education: Positions in higher education usually require PhD; others require masters or many years related experience.

Required Skill Sets: Subject matter expertise, public speaking skills, ability to organize and present material in an understandable manner.

Ongoing Training: The best instructors continue learning.

Career Particulars

Types of Organizations That Hire: Colleges,
corporations, educational publishers, adult education and training
providers. Try: *Career Education Corporation, Purple Monkey Studios
Inc., Columbia College, Roosevelt University.*

Job Titles: Professor, Teacher, Instructor

Salary Range: Adult Education Instructors: $31,999–$49,000;
University Professors: $86,000–$130,000

Professional Support

Professional Organizations: The Alliance for Computers
and Writing, Association of Teachers of Technical Writing, Journalism
in Education Association, Association for Education in Journalism and
Mass Communications, American Association of University Professors.

Professional Publications: *Writing, Writing That Works.*

Real seriousness in regard to writing is one of the two absolute necessities. The other, unfortunately, is talent,
—Ernest Hemingway

An absolute necessary part of a writer's equipment, almost as necessary as talent, is the ability to stand up under punishment, both the punishment the world hands out and the punishment he inflicts upon himself.
—Irwin Shaw

How can you know that something is worth writing about if you haven't seen anything else?
—Paul Theroux

To be a writer you need to see things as they are, and to see things as they are you need a certain basic innocence.
—Tobias Wolff

Appendix A: Professional Organizations

Academy of American Poets
The Academy is a nonprofit organization with a mission to support American poets at all stages of their careers and to foster the appreciation of contemporary poetry.
> 584 Broadway, Suite 604, New York, NY 10012-5243
> (212) 274 0343
> http://www.poets.org

Alliance for Computers and Writing
A national, non-profit organization committed to supporting teachers at all levels of computer-enhanced, computer-supported, and computer-based instruction
> http://www2.nau.edu/acw/

American Advertising Federation
The American Advertising Federation protects and promotes the well-being of advertising. We accomplish this through a unique, nationally coordinated grassroots network of advertisers, agencies, media companies, local advertising clubs and college chapters.
> 1101 Vermont Avenue, NW, Suite 500, Washington, DC 20005-6306
> (202) 898 0089
> http://www.aaf.org

American Association of University Professors
AAUP's purpose is to advance academic freedom and shared governance, to define fundamental professional values and standards for higher education, and to ensure higher education's contribution to the common good.
> 1012 Fourteenth Street, NW, Suite 500; Washington, DC 20005
> (202) 737 5900
> http://www.aaup.org

American Bankers Association
The American Bankers Association has been the premier voice of the
American banking industry for 125 years, with assets of member banks
representing approximately 90 percent of the industry total. ABA's
mission is twofold: to provide high-quality banking education and
training products and services, and to serve as the voice of the banking
industry.
> 1120 Connecticut Avenue, NW, Washington, DC 20036
> 1-800-BANKERS
> http://www.aba.org

American Crime Writers League
The ACWL was formed in the late 1980s by a group of writers who
wanted a private forum for exchanging ideas, complaining about almost
everything, and trying to understand this decidedly wacky business.
> http://www.acwl.org

American Marketing Association
For over six decades the AMA has been an essential resource
providing relevant marketing information that experienced marketers
turn to every day.
> 311 South Wacker Drive, Suite 5800, Chicago, IL 60606
> (800) AMA 1150
> http://www.marketingpower.com/

American Medical Writers Association
The mission of the American Medical Writers Association is to promote
excellence in medical communication and to provide educational
resources that support that goal.
> 40 West Gude Drive, Suite 101, Rockville, MD 20850-1192
> (301) 294 5303
> http://www.amwa.org

American Screenwriters Association
The American Screenwriters Association™ (ASA) is organized for
educational purposes, including the promotion and encouragement of
the art of screenwriting. ASA is committed to the international support
and advancement of all screenwriters. We welcome interested
individuals from around the world who are pursuing the writing of
documentaries, educational films, feature films, television, and even
radio and large screen format (Omnimax ™, IMAX ™) films.
> 269 South Beverly Drive, Suite 2600, Beverly Hills, CA 90212-
> 3807
> http://www.asascreenwriters.com/

American Society for Training and Development

ASTD (American Society for Training & Development) is the world's largest association dedicated to workplace learning and performance professionals.

1640 King Street, Box 1443, Alexandria, Virginia, 22313-2043
(703) 683 8100
http://www.astd.org

The American Society of Indexers

ASI is the only professional organization in the United States devoted solely to the advancement of indexing, abstracting, and database building.

10200 West 44th Avenue, Suite 304, Wheat Ridge, CO 80033
(303) 463 2887
http://www.asindexing.org

American Society of Journalists and Authors

The American Society of Journalists and Authors helps professional freelance writers advance their writing careers.

1501 Broadway, Suite 302, New York, NY 10036
(212) 997 0947
http://www.asja.org

American Society of Magazine Editors

The American Society of Magazine Editors (ASME) is the professional organization for editors of consumer magazines and business publications, which are edited, published and sold in the U.S.

810 Seventh Avenue, 24th Floor, New York, NY 10019
(212) 872 3700
http://www.magazine.org

Association for Education in Journalism and Mass Communications

The Association for Education in Journalism and Mass Communication is a non-profit, educational association of journalism and mass communication faculty, administrators, students and media professionals.

234 Outlet Pointe Blvd, Columbia, SC 29210-5667
(803) 798 0271
http://www.aejmc.org

Association for Women in Communications

The Association for Women in Communications is the one organization that recognizes the complex relationships that exist across communications disciplines. Modern communicators must demonstrate competence in varied disciplines and be able to network and make career moves across the broad spectrum of communications fields.

> 780 Ritchie Highway, Suite 28-S, Severna Park, MD 21146
> (410) 544 7442
> http://www.womcom.org

Association of Authors Representatives

The Association of Authors' Representatives, Inc. (AAR) is a not-for-profit organization of independent literary and dramatic agents. The AAR was formed in 1991 through the merger of the Society of Authors' Representatives (founded in 1928) and the Independent Literary Agents Association (founded in 1977).

> http://www.aar-online.org

Association of Teachers of Technical Writing

> http://www.attw.org

The Authors Guild

From 1919 on, the Guild has worked on behalf of its members to lobby for free speech, copyrights and other issues of concern to authors and bring authors the latest news in the publishing industry via the *Guild Bulletin*.

> 31 East 28th Street, 10th Floor, New York, NY 10016-7923
> (212) 563 5904
> http://www.authorsguild.org

Aviation/Space Writers Association

> 17 South High Street, Suite 1200, Columbus, OH 43215
> (614) 681 1900

Chicago Literary Club

The Club is a voluntary association of men and women interested in writing original essays on topics of their own choosing and in listening to other members present their essays. Meetings are held on Monday evenings from October through May; one essay is delivered each evening. Most members are not professional writers, but all are expected to express themselves competently in English, and to present their essays in typewritten or printed form to the Secretary for inclusion in the Club archives.

> www.chilit.org

Chicago Screenwriters Network
http://www.chicagoscreenwriters.org

Children's Book Council
The Children's Book Council, Inc. is the nonprofit trade association of publishers and packagers of trade books and related materials for children and young adults.
12 West 37th Street, 2nd Floor, New York, NY 10018-7480
(212) 966 1990
http://www.cbcbooks.org/

CineStory
National non-profit screenwriter's organization that helps emerging screenwriters
hone their craft and find alternative access to the screen.
PO Box 3736, Idyllwild, CA 92549
(909) 659 1180
http://www.cinestory.com

Council of Public Relations Firms
317 Madison Avenue, Suite 2320, New York, NY 10017
(877) 773 4767)
http://www.prfirms.org/

The Dramatists Guild of America
Professional association of American playwrights. The Guild protects the rights
of dramatists in relation to producers and more recently Directors.
1501 Broadway, Suite 701, New York, NY 10036
(212) 398 9366
http://www.dramaguild.com

Editorial Freelance Association
The Editorial Freelancers Association is a national, nonprofit, professional organization of self-employed workers in the publishing and communications industries. Members are editors, writers, indexers, proofreaders, researchers, desktop publishers, translators, and others who offer a broad range of skills and specialties.
71 West 23rd Street, Suite 1910, New York, NY 10010-4181
(866) 929 5400
www.the-efa.org

Financial Women International
Financial Women International, Inc. (formerly the National Association of Bank Women) was founded in 1921—one year after women won the right to vote-by a group of New York City women bankers. FWI serves women in the financial services industry who seek to expand their personal and professional capabilities through self-directed growth in a supportive environment.
> 1027 West Roselawn Avenue
> Roseville, MN 55113
> (866) 236 2007
> http://www.fwi.org

Garden Writers Association
The Garden Writers Association (GWA) is an organization of over 1800 professional communicators in the lawn and garden industry. No other organization in the industry has as much direct contact with the buying public as GWA.
> 10210 Leatherleaf Court, Manassas, VA 20111
> (703) 257 1032
> http://www.gardenwriters.org/

Horror Writers of America
HWA is a worldwide organization of writers and publishing professionals dedicated to promoting dark literature and the interests of those who write it. HWA was formed in the late 1980s with the help of many of the field's greats, including Dean Koontz, Robert McCammon, and Joe Lansdale. Today, with over 1,000 members around the globe, it is the oldest and most respected professional organization for the much-loved writers who bring you the most enjoyable sleepless nights of your life.
> PO Box 50577, Palo Alto, CA 94303
> http://www.horror.org

Illinois Women's Press Association
Association of communications professionals working in newspaper, radio, television,
public relations, marketing, advertising, and related media.
> PO Box 59256, Schaumburg, IL 60159-0256
> (312) 458 9151
> http://www.iwpa.org

Independent Writers of Chicago
IWOC is a nonprofit professional association of freelance writers who work primarily throughout the Chicago metropolitan area. IWOC members serve large corporations, small businesses, and not-for-profit organizations; together they represent a broad range of writing talents and specialties.

> PMB 119 5465 West Grand Avenue, Suite 100, Gurnee, IL 60031
> (847) 855 6670
> http://www.iwoc.org

International Association of Business Communicators
IABC is a not-for-profit international network of professionals committed to improving the effectiveness of organizations through strategic interactive and integrated business communication management.

> One Hallidie Plaza, Suite 600 San Francisco, CA 94102
> (415) 544 4700
> http://www.iabc.com

International Food, Wine, and Travel Writers Association
The International Food Wine and Travel Writers Association (IFW&TWA) strives to be a gathering point and resource base for an active membership composed of professionals engaged in the food, wine and travel industries. The association's membership includes professionals in culinary arts and sciences, the wine growing and production industry, and in the hotel and hospitality management industries.

> 1142 South Diamond Bar Boulevard, #177, Diamond Bar, CA 91765
> (877) 439 8929
> http://www.ifwtwa.org

International Platform Association
For those interested in lecturing and public speaking. Members take an active interest in vital world issues. In the ancient tradition of lecture platform it brings people, ideas, and issues together for open and free discourse. Annual convention provides a central marketplace for speakers, diversified audiences, and those who engage speakers.

> PO Box 250, Winnetka, IL 60093
> (847) 446 4321
> http://www.internationalplatform.com

International Webmaster Association
Global leader for advancing the web professional.
    119 East Union Street. Suite #F, Pasadena, CA 91103
    (626) 449 3709
    http://www.iwanet.org

International Women's Writing Guild
The IWWG, founded in 1976, is a network for the personal and
professional empowerment of women through writing and open to all
regardless of portfolio.
    PO Box 810, Gracie Station, New York, NY 10028-0082
    (212) 737 7536
    www.iwwg.com

Journalism Education Association
The Journalism Education Association supports free and responsible
scholastic journalism by providing resources and educational
opportunities, by promoting professionalism, by encouraging and
rewarding student excellence and teacher achievement, and by
fostering an atmosphere which encompasses diversity yet builds unity.
    Kansas State University, 103 Kedzie Hall, Manhattan, KS
    66506-1505
    (785) 532 5532
    http://www.jea.org

Mystery Writers of America
Mystery Writers of America is the premier organization for mystery
writers, professionals allied to the crime writing field, aspiring crime
writers, and those who are devoted to the genre. MWA is dedicated to
promoting higher regard for crime writing and recognition and respect
for those who write within the genre.
    17 East 47th Street, 6th Floor, New York NY 10017
    (212) 888 8171
    http://www.mysterywriters.org/

National Association of Government Communicators
The National Association of Government Communicators (NAGC) is a
national not-for-profit professional network of federal, state and local
government employees who disseminate information within and outside
government. Its members are editors, writers, graphic artists, video
professionals, broadcasters, photographers, information specialists and
agency spokespersons.
    10366 Democracy Lane, Suite B, Fairfax, VA 22030
    (703) 691 0377
    http://www.nagc.com

National Association of Professional Environmental Communicators (NAPEC)
PO Box 61-8352, Chicago IL 60661-8352
(312) 661 1721

National Association of Science Writers
The mission of NASW is to "foster the dissemination of accurate information regarding science through all media normally devoted to informing the public."
PO Box 890, Hedgesville, WV 25427
(304) 754 5077
http://www.nasw.org

National Book Critics Circle
360 Park Avenue South, New York, NY 10010
http://www.bookcritics.org/

National Speakers Association
The National Speakers Association (NSA) is the leading organization for those who speak professionally. NSA's 3,500 members include experts in a variety of industries and disciplines, who reach audiences as trainers, educators, humorists, motivators, consultants, authors and more. Since 1973, NSA has provided resources and education designed to advance the skills, integrity and value of its members and speaking profession.
1500 South Priest Drive, Tempe, AZ 85281
(480) 968 2552
http://www.nsaspeaker.org/

National Writers Union
NWU is the trade union for freelance writers of all genres. We are committed to improving the economic and working conditions of freelance writers through the collective strength of our members. We offer contract advice and grievance resolution, member education, job banks, networking, social and professional events, and much more. The NWU is affiliated with the United Automobile Workers (UAW) and through them with the AFL-CIO. Founded in 1983, the NWU has locals, organizing committees and genre divisions throughout the country. Our thousands of members include journalists, book authors, poets, copywriters, academic authors, cartoonists, and technical and business writers.
113 University Place, 6th Floor, New York, NY 10003
(212) 254 0279
http://www.nwu.org

Newspaper Association of America
NAA is a nonprofit organization representing the $55 billion newspaper industry. NAA members account for nearly 90 percent of the daily circulation in the United States and a wide range of non-daily U.S. newspapers. NAA also has many Canadian and International members. Educators, university newspapers, press associations and suppliers/vendors also are members. The Association focuses on six key strategic priorities that collectively affect the newspaper industry: marketing, public policy, diversity, industry development, newspaper operations and readership.
>1921 Gallows Road, Suite 600, Vienna, VA 22182-3900
>(703) 902 1600
>http://www.naa.org

Outdoor Writers Association of America
Our mission is to improve the professional skills of our members, set the highest ethical and communications standards, encourage public enjoyment and conservation of natural resources, and mentor the next generation of professional outdoor communicators.
>121 Hickory Street, Suite 1, Missoula, MT 59801
>(406) 728 7434
>http://www.owaa.org

PEN America
PEN American Center is the largest of the 141 centers of International PEN, the world's oldest human rights organization and the oldest international literary organization. International PEN was founded in 1921 to dispel national, ethnic, and racial hatreds and to promote understanding among all countries. PEN American Center, founded a year later, works to advance literature, to defend free expression, and to foster international literary fellowship.
>588 Broadway, Suite 303, New York, NY 10012
>(212) 334 1660
>http://www.pen.org

Poetry Center of Chicago
>37 South Wabash Avenue, Chicago, IL 60603
>(312) 899 1229
>http://www.poetrycenter.org

The Poetry Club
This is not just a community of writers it is a community of people from the entire world and their writing has made them one. They think of themselves as family a close tight family that will welcome any one into the PCLA home. The changes we have made over the years are vital to help the community continue to grow and flourish the way it needs.
>http://www.poetryclub.com/

Professional Association of Résumé Writers

The Professional Association of Résumé Writers & Career Coaches was founded in January of 1990. Prior to that time, there had been no association for career professionals to exchange information, enhance their skills, or demonstrate their commitment to providing professional services to the general public. Today, those who display the association's logo affirm their dedication to excellence in meeting client career goals. In addition, many members then choose to seek certification to further affirm their expertise as career professionals.

    1388 Brightwaters Boulevard, NE, St. Petersburg, FL 33704
    (800) 822 7279
    http://www.parw.com

Professional Résumé Writing & Research Association

The Professional Résumé Writing and Research Association (PRWRA) is an innovative organization which places membership benefits as its highest priority. The goal of PRWRA is to increase member knowledge and income.

    (888) 86-PRWRA (867-7972)
    http://www.prwra.com/

Public Relations Society of America

PRSA is the world's largest organization for public relations professionals. Its nearly 20,000 members, organized into 114 chapters, represent business and industry, technology, counseling firms, government, associations, hospitals, schools, professional services firms and nonprofit organizations.

    33 Maiden Lane, 11th Floor, New York, NY 10038-5150
    (212) 460 1400
    http://www.prsa.org/

Publicity Club of Chicago

PCC is the practical resource for providing the tools, technology and tactics Chicago-area professional communicators need to implement high-quality communications programs and to excel in public relations.

    PO Box 10916, Chicago, IL 60610
    (773) 463 5560
    www.publicity.org

Romance Writers of America

Romance Writers of America is the professional association for 9,000 published and aspiring romance writers. Members of RWA write the novels that make up 48% of all popular paperback fiction and that generate more than $1 billion in sales each year.

> 16000 Stuebner Airline Road, Suite 140, Spring, TX 77379
> (832) 717 5200
> www.rwanational.com

Science Fiction & Fantasy Writers

SFWA[SM] has brought together the most successful and daring writers of speculative fiction throughout the world, and has grown in numbers and influence until it is now widely recognized as one of the most effective non-profit writers' organizations in existence. Over 1200 science fiction and fantasy writers, artists, editors, and allied professionals are members.

> http://www.sfwa.org

Science Fiction Poetry Association

The Science Fiction Poetry Association was founded in 1978 to bring together poets and readers interested in science fiction poetry.

> Mike Allen, SFPA President, 3514 Signal Hill Ave NW,
> Roanoke VA 24017
> www.sfpoetry.com

The Scriptwriters Network

Founded in 1986, The Scriptwriters Network is a non-profit, volunteer-based organization created by writers for writers. The Network serves its members by enhancing their awareness of the realities of the business, providing access and opportunity through alliances with industry professionals, and furthering the cause and quality of writing in the entertainment industry..

> http://www.scriptwritersnetwork.com

Society for Technical Communication

STC is an individual membership organization dedicated to advancing the arts and sciences of technical communication. It is the largest organization of its type in the world. Its 18,000 members include technical writers and editors, content developers, documentation specialists, technical illustrators, instructional designers, academics, information architects, usability and human factors professionals, visual designers, Web designers and developers, and translators.

> 901 North Stuart Street, Suite 904, Arlington, VA 22203
> (703) 522 4114
> http://www.stc.org

Society of American Business Editors and Writers
The Society of American Business Editors and Writers Inc. is a not-for-profit organization made up of business journalists in North America.
> Missouri School of Journalism, 134 Neff Annex, Columbia, MO
> 65211-1200
> (573) 882 7862
> http://www.sabew.org

Society of Children's Book Writers & Illustrators
The Society of Children's Book Writers and Illustrators, formed in 1971 by a group of Los Angeles based writers for children, is the only international organization to offer a variety of services to people who write, illustrate, or share a vital interest in children's literature. The SCBWI acts as a network for the exchange of knowledge between writers, illustrators, editors, publishers, agents, librarians, educators, booksellers and others involved with literature for young people.
> 8271 Beverly Boulevard, Los Angeles, CA 90048
> (323) 782 1010
> http://www.scbwi.org

Society of Midland Authors
> PO Box 10419, Chicago, IL 60610
> http://www.midlandauthors.com

Society of Professional Journalists
The Society of Professional Journalists is dedicated to the perpetuation of a free press as the cornerstone of our nation and our liberty.
> 3909 North Meridian Street, Indianapolis, IN 46208
> (317) 927 8000
> http://www.spj.org/

Toastmasters International
At Toastmasters, members learn by speaking to groups and working with others in a supportive environment. A typical Toastmasters club is made up of 20 to 30 people who meet once a week for about an hour. Each meeting gives everyone an opportunity to practice.
> http://www.toastmasters.org

Webgrrls
Webgrrls is a networking and mentoring forum for women in or interested in new
media or technology.
> http://www.webgrrls.com

Women's National Book Association
The Women's National Book Association is a national organization of women and men who work with and value books. WNBA exists to promote reading and to support the role of women in the community of the book.

     c/o Susannah Greenberg Public Relations, 2166 Broadway, #9-E, New York, NY 10024
     (212) 208 4629
     http://www.wnba-books.org

Women's New Media Alliance
Wise-Women is a world-wide, online community of web designers, developers and programmers.

     http://www.wnma.org

Appendix B: Online Job Resources

BrassRing: http://www.brassring.com/
Technical writing jobs...

Business Marketing Associates Chicago:
http://www.bmachicago.org/careerlink.lasso
Writers, designers, and other creatives with a flair for marketing...

CareerBuilder: http://www.careerbuilder.com/_
Jobs of all kinds...

CareerJournal.com: http://www.careerjournal.com/
The Wall Street Journal's Executive Career Site...

CareerMole.com: http://careermole.com/
Search jobs of all kinds in and out of the area...

Chicago Headline Club Jobs: http://www.headlineclub.org/jobs/
Print, television, radio, and other broadcast jobs in Chicagoland...

College Grad Job Hunter: http://www.collegegrad.com/
Entry-level jobs for college grads...

Computer Jobs: http://www.computerjobs.com/
Technical writing and web jobs for Chicago and other major metro areas...

CopyDesk: http://www.copydesk.net/
An outsourcing and placement agency that specializes in working with writers, editors, and proofreaders...

Crain Communications, Inc. Job Postings:
http://www.crain.com/c_emp/HRSearch.cfm
HR Department job postings for Chicago and other Crain offices...

Dice.com: http://www.dice.com/
Technical writing jobs across the country...

Editor & Publisher Jobs:
http://www.editorandpublisher.com/eandp/classifieds/index.jsp
Newspaper industry jobs around the country...

EditorJobs.com: http://www.editorjobs.com/
Fulltime and freelance editing positions of all kinds...

Freelance Opportunities: http://www.freelancewriting.com/fjb.html
Freelance jobs and market news...

Employment Guide: http://www.employmentguide.com/
Variety of jobs, career advice, and work-at-home opportunities...

Lynn Hazan & Associates: http://www.lhazan.com/
The latest job openings from this Chicago recruiter...

HotJobs.com: http://www.hotjobs.com/htdocs/channels/arts/
Rival of the famous Monster.com site, HotJobs was recently purchased by Yahoo!, so its arts and publishing job search engine lives on...

Literary Publishing Jobs:
http://www.clmp.org/jobs/job_search_form.html
Job listings from the Council of Literary Magazines and Presses...

Magazine Job Bank:
http://www.magazine.org/Editorial/MPA_ASME_Job_Bank/
American Society of Magazine Editors job bank...

Media Bistro: http://www.mediabistro.com/joblistings/
Where creatives meet opportunities...

Monster.com: http://jobsearch.monster.com/
The mega job search site with over 1,000,000 listings on any given day, including category and keyword searches...

NAA Newspaper Career Bank:
http://www.naa.org/classified/index.html
Newspaper Association of America job bank...

NationJob.com: http://www.nationjob.com/
Job search engine for careers across the country...

National Writers Union Job Hotline: http://www.nwu.org/hotline
One of the largest writing groups on the planet...

Net Temps: http://www.net-temps.com/regional/state.html
Temporary, contract, and fulltime jobs throughout the country...

Newsjobs Network: http://www.newsjobs.net/usa/
Comprehensive listing of employment sites for writers...

Paying Markets for Freelancers: http://www.writerswrite.com/paying/
Updated market information for freelance writers...

Pif Magazine Writers Only: http://pifmagazine.com/writers_only/
Classified ads for writers and publishers...

Publisher's Lunch Job Board:
http://click.email-publisher.com/maacxaOaa84DPa5bFT7baeQxXH/
Fulltime and temporary publishing positions of all levels...

Reed Business Information Jobs:
http://www.reedbusiness.com/index.asp?layout=inside&articleId=CA15
0198
Magazine opportunities at Reed publications...

Society for Scholarly Publishing: http://sspnet.org/
Job postings around the country for experienced publishing professionals...

Sun Consultants: http://www.sunconsultants.com/
Specializing in placing highly qualified mid- to senior-level advertising, design, and Web professionals...

SunOasis: http://www.sunoasis.com/
Job postings for writers, editors, and copywriters...

Telecommuting Jobs for Writers:
http://216.71.194.152/new/writers.shtml
Job opportunities available with no commute necessary...

True Careers: http://www.careercity.com/
Job listings and career advice for educated professionals...

Webgrrls: http://www.webgrrls.com/jobbank/
Job postings for online writers, editors, and other Web professionals...

The Write Jobs: http://www.writerswrite.net/joblist.cfm
Local and national full-time and freelance job listings...

Write.ms: http://www.poewar.com/jobs/
Job postings around the country for writers and editors...

Writers Weekly: http://www.writersweekly.com/
Freelance job listings and new paying markets...

Appendix C: More Sample Salaries

MediaBistro Salary Survey for the Midwest
For more information, go to ttp://www.mediabistro.com/salarysurvey/?c=mbenag

• Salaries By Industries	25th Percentile (25% Earn Less)	50th Percentile (50% Earn Less)	75th Percentile (75% Earn Less)	Number Responding
TOTAL	$30,000	$40,000	$55,000	938
Advertising - other	$29,000	$32,000	$39,000	13
Advertising: agency	$28,000	$35,000	$45,500	53
Association publication	$30,000	$41,000	$50,400	20
Book publishing - other	$32,275	$40,000	$52,000	26
Book publishing: consumer	$27,810	$40,000	$55,000	36
Book publishing: trade/B2B	$32,000	$40,000	$55,000	18
Magazine: large consumer/national	$36,000	$47,500	$65,000	64
Magazine: local/regional	$28,000	$33,000	$45,000	66
Magazine: trade magazines/B2B pub.	$33,660	$43,000	$60,714	110
Marketing (in-house): Fortune 1000	$34,320	$41,000	$61,200	16
Marketing (in-house): small/mid-sized	$34,000	$45,000	$52,000	27
Newspaper: community	$22,000	$24,500	$32,000	46
Newspaper: local/regional	$27,300	$36,000	$48,000	123
Newspaper: national	$50,000	$55,000	$57,700	10
Online/new media	$40,000	$53,000	$72,000	43
Other, specify	$34,000	$42,500	$58,000	63
PR (firm): Fortune 1000 clients	$19,200	$32,000	$55,000	13
PR (firm): small/mid-sized clients	$29,500	$35,000	$48,000	19
PR (in-house): small/mid-sized	$36,000	$49,000	$70,000	27
Pr/marketing - other	$34,000	$42,000	$50,000	26
Print - other	$33,000	$43,000	$52,000	16
TV: news (local)	$25,000	$30,000	$43,500	20
Wire Service	$42,000	$50,000	$77,000	10

MediaBistro Freelance Data

For more information, go to
http://www.mediabistro.com/salarysurvey/default_freelance_data.asp?c=mbenag

Salaries By Category	25th Percentile (25% Earn Less)	50th Percentile (50% Earn Less)	75th Percentile (75% Earn Less)	Number Responding
TOTAL	$17,400	$35,000	$60,000	3179
Region				
Northeast	$20,000	$40,000	$65,000	1613
West	$18,000	$39,000	$60,000	673
South	$10,000	$28,000	$50,000	457
Midwest	$10,000	$30,000	$55,000	241
Metro Area				
New York-Newark-Edison, NY-NJ-PA	$24,000	$40,000	$65,000	1293
Los Angeles-Long Beach-Santa Ana, CA	$20,000	$40,000	$70,000	286
San Francisco-Oakland-Fremont, CA	$30,000	$40,000	$65,000	124
Washington-Arlington-Alexandria, DC-VA-MD-WV	$20,000	$38,000	$53,760	123
Chicago-Naperville-Joliet, IL-IN-WI	$15,000	$35,000	$55,000	111
Boston-Cambridge-Quincy, MA-NH	$10,000	$30,000	$49,000	89
Philadelphia-Camden-Wilmington, PA-NJ-DE-MD	$14,000	$35,000	$70,000	73
Seattle-Tacoma-Bellevue, WA	$16,000	$40,000	$54,000	55
Atlanta-Sandy Springs-Marietta, GA	$5,000	$22,000	$34,000	43
Dallas-Fort Worth-Arlington, TX	$15,000	$35,000	$55,000	39
Bridgeport-Stamford-Norwalk, CT	$13,000	$42,000	$52,000	30
Miami-Fort Lauderdale-Miami Beach, FL	$22,000	$30,000	$70,000	29
Baltimore-Towson, MD	$5,500	$28,000	$50,000	26
San Diego-Carlsbad-San Marcos, CA	$5,000	$25,000	$50,000	21
Houston-Baytown-Sugar Land,	$9,500	$20,000	$34,000	20

TX

Denver-Aurora, CO	$18,000	$35,000	$56,000	18
Portland-Vancouver-Beaverton, OR-WA	$10,000	$20,000	$24,000	16
Detroit-Warren-Livonia, MI	$9,000	$43,000	$60,000	15
Phoenix-Mesa-Scottsdale, AZ	$10,000	$50,000	$76,000	15
Orlando, FL	$20,000	$35,000	$60,000	13
New Haven-Milford, CT	$10,400	$25,000	$42,000	12
New Orleans-Metairie-Kenner, LA	$2,000	$8,000	$22,000	11
Nashville-Davidson--Murfreesboro, TN	$2,600	$13,000	$20,100	11
Las Vegas-Paradise, NV	$5,000	$25,000	$72,000	11
Tampa-St. Petersburg-Clearwater, FL	$5,000	$25,000	$33,000	11
Austin-Round Rock, TX	$12,000	$25,000	$36,000	11
Minneapolis-St. Paul-Bloomington, MN-WI	$400	$10,000	$45,000	10

Salaries By Category	25th Percentile (25% Earn Less)	50th Percentile (50% Earn Less)	75th Percentile (75% Earn Less)	Number Responding
Madison, WI	$2,400	$20,500	$50,000	10
Boulder, CO	$6,000	$30,000	$55,000	10

Expertise

Salaries By Category	25th Percentile (25% Earn Less)	50th Percentile (50% Earn Less)	75th Percentile (75% Earn Less)	Number Responding
Account Manager	$30,000	$50,000	$80,000	66
Art Director	$40,000	$70,000	$90,000	78
Book Author	$20,000	$40,000	$60,000	73
Cameraperson	$4,000	$26,000	$75,000	13
Content Editor (online)	$25,000	$45,000	$50,000	27
Coordinator (production)	$27,000	$40,000	$60,000	29
Coordinator (PR/marketing)	$12,000	$30,000	$43,000	21
Copy Editor	$15,000	$26,000	$40,000	143
Copywriter	$22,000	$40,000	$75,000	123
Designer	$25,000	$40,000	$65,000	39
Director	$25,000	$70,000	$95,000	27
Editor	$25,000	$40,000	$61,000	176
Editor (photo, picture)	$30,000	$40,000	$64,000	32
Editor (video, film)	$32,000	$60,000	$78,000	39
Fact-Checker	$15,000	$35,000	$41,000	26
Graphic Designer	$25,000	$40,000	$55,000	133
Illustrator	$25,000	$35,000	$85,000	12
Photographer	$15,000	$27,000	$45,000	75
Producer (new media)	$50,000	$72,000	$110,000	26
Producer (television)	$35,000	$50,000	$78,000	206
Production (print)	$27,000	$50,000	$72,000	29
Promotions	$25,000	$40,000	$65,000	57
Publisher	$40,000	$56,000	$105,000	10
Reporter	$11,660	$25,000	$45,000	236
Researcher	$7,200	$10,000	$39,000	17
Sales Person	$12,000	$38,000	$48,000	10
Technical Writer	$20,000	$40,000	$78,000	53
Web Designer	$13,000	$35,000	$62,000	43
Web Developer	$8,000	$50,000	$60,000	15
Writer	$10,000	$30,000	$50,000	1032
Other	$20,000	$40,000	$70,000	275

Salaries By Category	25th Percentile (25% Earn Less)	50th Percentile (50% Earn Less)	75th Percentile (75% Earn Less)	Number Responding
Industry				
Advertising: agency	$33,000	$50,000	$72,000	131
Advertising: client side	$20,000	$40,000	$85,000	34
Advertising - other	$25,000	$40,000	$60,000	47
Association publication	$18,000	$35,000	$50,000	22
Book publishing: consumer	$16,000	$35,000	$60,000	146
Book publishing: trade/B2B	$20,000	$36,000	$55,000	74
Book publishing - other	$15,000	$35,000	$48,000	79
Cable: entertainment (national)	$40,000	$60,000	$80,000	73
Cable: news (national)	$30,000	$45,000	$65,000	19
Film: documentary	$15,000	$40,000	$50,000	23
Film: independent	$10,000	$30,000	$48,000	33
Film: mainstream	$10,000	$35,000	$70,000	26
Magazine: large consumer/national	$25,000	$40,000	$60,000	575
Magazine: local/regional	$5,100	$20,000	$30,000	194
Magazine: trade magazines/B2B pub.	$20,000	$35,000	$55,000	206
Marketing (firm): Fortune 1000 clients	$7,000	$37,000	$75,000	18
Marketing (firm): small/mid-sized clients	$25,000	$38,000	$95,000	25
Marketing (in-house): Fortune 1000	$31,000	$66,000	$80,000	23
Marketing (in-house): small/mid-sized	$15,000	$30,000	$48,000	29
Newsletter: consumer	$5,000	$30,000	$60,000	12
Newsletter: trade	$9,000	$30,000	$36,000	28
Newspaper: community	$2,000	$10,000	$20,000	30
Newspaper: local/regional	$3,000	$13,000	$25,000	173
Newspaper: national	$12,500	$35,000	$50,000	89
Print - other	$18,000	$35,000	$55,000	103
Online/new media	$15,000	$35,000	$56,000	219

PR (firm): Fortune 1000 clients	$36,000	$75,000	$83,000	11
PR (firm): small/mid-sized clients	$30,000	$45,000	$65,000	31
PR (in-house): small/mid-sized	$15,000	$35,000	$50,000	16
Pr/marketing - other	$30,000	$50,000	$75,000	94
Professional journal	$10,000	$30,000	$51,000	24
Radio: entertainment (national)	$1,200	$15,000	$18,000	11
TV: entertainment (local)	$12,000	$30,000	$32,000	11
TV: entertainment (national)	$30,000	$50,000	$75,000	134
TV: news (local)	$15,000	$32,000	$55,000	23
TV: news (national)	$38,000	$65,000	$83,000	45
Broadcasting - other	$20,000	$35,000	$50,000	34
Wire Service	$12,000	$27,000	$42,000	15
Other	$16,000	$40,000	$70,000	245

Salaries By Category	25th Percentile (25% Earn Less)	50th Percentile (50% Earn Less)	75th Percentile (75% Earn Less)	Number Responding
Client Type				
Local/Regional	$10,000	$24,500	$40,000	982
National	$25,000	$40,000	$65,000	1742
International	$25,000	$45,000	$70,000	454
Years of Experience				
Entry Level	$1,000	$10,000	$25,000	136
1-2 Years	$5,000	$18,000	$33,000	269
3-5 Years	$15,000	$30,000	$47,000	618
6-10 Years	$20,000	$40,000	$60,000	874
11-15 Years	$25,000	$50,000	$75,000	526
15+ Years	$25,000	$48,000	$75,000	965
Annual Earnings				
2003 Earnings	$10,000	$30,000	$52,000	3179
2004 Earnings	$17,400	$35,000	$60,000	3179
2005 Earnings (projected), compared to 2004:				
More than 2004				2045
Less than 2004				235
Same as 2004				899

WritersMarket.com Freelance Fees

For more information, go to http://www.writersmarket.com/content/howmuch8.asp.

Magazines & Trade Journals

Abstracting: $20-30/hour for trade and professional journals; $20 low, $30 mid-range, $60 high/hour for scholarly journals.

Advertorial: $650, low; $1,000 high/printed page.

Article manuscript critique: $40/3,000 words.

Arts reviewing: $35-100 flat fee or 20-30¢/word, plus admission to events or copy of CD (for music).

Book reviews: $22, low; $50, mid-range, $175 high, $750 very high/piece; 25¢-$1/word.

Consultation on magazine editorial: $1,000-1,500/day plus expenses.

Copyediting magazines: $16-30/hour.

Editing: General, $25-500/day or $250-2,000/issue; Religious publications, $200-500/month or $15-30/hour.

Fact checking: $26 low, $50 mid-range, $75 high/hour.

Feature articles: Anywhere from 20¢ to $4/word; or $150-2,750 per 1,500 word article, depending on size (circulation) and reputation of magazine.

Ghostwriting articles (general): Up to $2/word; or $300-3,000/project.

Indexing: $15-40/hour.

Magazine, city, calendar of events column: $50-150/column.

Magazine column: 25¢ low, $1.50 mid-range, $4 high/word; $25 low, $200 mid-range, $2,500 high/piece. Larger publications pay fees related to their regular word rate.

Magazine copyediting: $15, low; $25, mid-range, $50 high, $100 very high/hour.

Magazine editing: $15, low; $30, mid-range, $60 high/hour.

Magazine research: $20, low; $40, mid-range, $75 high/hour.

Manuscript consultation: $25-50/hour.

Manuscript criticism: $40-60 per article or short story of up to 3,000 words. Also $20-25/hour.

Permission fees to publishers to reprint article or story: $75-500; 10-15¢/word; less for charitable organizations.

Production editing: $15-30/hour.

Proofreading: $12-25/hour.

Research: $20-25/hour.

Rewriting: Up to $80/manuscript page; also $100/published page.

Science writing for magazines: $2,000-5,000/article.

Special news article: For a business's submission to trade publication, $250-500 for 1,000 words.

Stringing: 20¢ to $1/word based on circulation. Daily rate: $150-250 plus expenses; weekly rate: $900 plus expenses. Also $10-35/hour plus expenses; $1/column inch.

Trade journal feature article: For business client, $400-1,000. Also $1-2/word.

Newspapers

Ads for small business: $25 for a small, one-column ad, or $10/hour and up

Arts reviewing: For weekly newspapers, $15-50 flat fee; for dailies, $50 and up; for Sunday supplements, $100-400. Also admission to event or copy of CD (for music).

Book reviews: For small newspapers, byline and the book only; for larger publications, $35-200 and a copy of the book.

Column, local: $40, low; $125, mid-range; $300 high/hour, depending on circulation.

Copyediting: $10-30/hour; up to $40/hour for large daily paper.

Dance criticism: $25-400/article.

Drama criticism: Local, newspaper rates; non-local, $50 and up per review.

Editing/manuscript evaluation: $25/hour.

Feature: $25, low; $200, mid-range; $500 high/piece, depending on circulation. In Canada 15-40 ¢/word, but rates vary widely.

Obituary copy: Where local newspapers permit lengthier than normal notices paid for by the funeral home (and charged to the family), $15-25. Writers are engaged by funeral homes.

Proofreading: $16-20/hour.

Reporting: $25, low; $45, mid-range; $100 high/piece (small circulation); $60, low; $175, high/piece (large circulation).

Stringing: $10, low; $25, mid-range; $40 high/piece; $1/column inch, sometimes with additional mileage payment .

Syndicated column, self-promoted: $5-10 each for weeklies; $10-25/week for dailies, based on circulation.

Miscellaneous

Comedy writing for night club entertainers: Gags only, $5-25 each. Routines, $100-1,000 per minute. Some new comics may try to get a 5-minute routine for $150; others will pay $2,500 for a 5-minute bit from a top writer.

Comics writing: $35-50/page and up for established comics writers.

Contest judging: Short manuscripts, $10/entry; with one-page critique, $15-25. Overall contest judging: $100-500.

Corporate comedy skits: $300-800 for half-hour skit (used at meetings, conventions).

Craft ideas with instructions: $50-200/project.

Encyclopedia articles: Entries in some reference books, such as biographical encyclopedias, 500-2,000 words; pay ranges from $60-80 per 1,000 words. Specialists' fees vary.

Family histories: Fees depend on whether the writer edits already prepared notes or does extensive research and writing; and the length of the work, $500-15,000.

Institutional (church, school) history: $200-1,000 for 15-50 pages, or $20-35/hour.

Manuscript typing: Depending on manuscript length and delivery schedule, $1.25-2/page with one copy; $15/hour.

Party toasts, limericks, place card verses: $1.50/line.

Research for individuals: $5-30/hour, depending on experience, geographic area and nature of work.

Special occasion booklet: Family keepsake of a wedding, anniversary, Bar Mitzvah, etc., $120 and up.

ChicagoWriter.com
For and about the business of writing.

Here's some of what you'll find on ChicagoWriter.com:

Writers on Writing ● Word Wrangles
Superior Vocabulary Builders

ChicagoWriter Date Book

Clients in Focus ● Webliography ● Legal Briefs

Job Links ● Salary Wizard ● Career Services

We're the online resource for Chicago's
writers, editors, and publishing professionals.

Chicago Writer **Books**

Name: _____

Address: _____

City: _____ State: _____ ZIP: _____

Telephone: _____

Email Address: _____

Payment: ☐ Check or Money Order   ☐ VISA   ☐ MasterCard

Card Number: _____ Exp Date: ____ / ____ Verification Code: _____

Name: _____ Signature: _____

Billing Address: _____

City: _____ State: _____ ZIP: _____

# Copies	Title	Price Each	Total
	A Guide to Chicago Book Publishers, 5th Edition (ISBN 978-1-933048-37-6)	$40.00	
	A Guide to Chicagoland Magazines, 2nd Edition (ISBN 978-1-933048-26-0)	$44.95	
	A Guide to Writing Jobs in Chicago, 3e (ISBN 978-1-933048-35-2)	$19.95	
	A Guide to Chicago's Multicultural Publishers, 2nd Edition (ISBN 978-1-933048-28-4)	$34.95	
	Please add 8.75% sales tax for all orders shipped to Illinois addresses.	Sales Tax	
	Standard shipping is free. To upgrade to USPS Priority Mail, add $4.00 for the first book and $1.00 for each additional book.	Shipping	
	TOTAL DUE		$

Prices listed include free standard shipping to one location. All orders must be prepaid. Please remit order request along with credit card, check, or money order in $US to:

iWrite Publications Inc.
PO Box 10923
Chicago, Illinois 60610-0923

or fax your order toll free to
(888) 659 2882